The
Win Without Pitching
Manifesto

by Blair Enns

GEGEN PRESS | KASLO | 2018

For The People Who See,
so their enterprise may sustain their creativity

and for Colette, habibti

Gegen Press

PO Box 454

Kaslo BC V0G 1M0

Printed in the United States of America

First Edition Published 2010

Second Edition Published 2018, Third Printing 2021

ISBN-13: 978-1-9995235-0-3 (cloth)

ISBN-13: 978-1-9995235-2-7 (EPUB)

ISBN-13: 978-1-9995235-1-0 (MOBI)

pitch (verb)

[pĭch] To attempt to sell or win approval for one's ideas by giving them away for free, usually within a competitive, buyer-driven process

A Manifesto of Business Practices
for Creative Firms

The forces of the creative professions are aligned against the artist. These forces pressure him to give his work away for free as a means of proving his worthiness of the assignment. Clients demand it. Designers, art directors, writers and other creative professionals resign themselves to it. Trade associations are powerless against it. Consultants and outsourced business development firms earn their living by perpetuating it. And conferences put the worst offenders from all sides on stage and have them preach about how to get better at it.

It is a mistake to look to the creative professions to deal with this issue. Free pitching and speculative creative will only be beaten one firm at a time, with little help and much loud opposition from the professions themselves. This battle is but a collection of individual struggles: the single artist or creative firm against the many allied forces of the status quo.

But while collectively the battle may seem lost, a revolution is afoot. Some creative firms are fighting and winning. They are reclaiming the high ground in the client relationship, beating back the pitch and winning new business without first having to part with their thinking for free. They are building stronger practices amid the forces of commoditization.

This treatise contains the twelve proclamations of a Win Without Pitching firm. It describes a trail blazed by owners of creative businesses who have made the difficult business decisions and transformed their firms, and the way they go about getting new business. They have resisted the profession-wide pressure to toe the free-pitching line. They have gone from order-taker suppliers to expert advisors and have forged a more satisfying and lucrative way of getting and doing business.

Their path, described in these pages, may not be your path. Not everyone has the heart or stomach for revolution. It is up to you to read and decide for yourself if you will follow.

Blair Enns,
Kaslo

"Whenever you find yourself on the side of the majority,
it is time to pause and reflect."
Mark Twain

{ The Twelve Proclamations }

I

We Will Specialize

We will acknowledge that it is the availability of substitutes – the legitimate alternatives to the offerings of our firm – that allows the client to ask, and compels us to give, our thinking away for free. If we are not seen as more expert than our competition then we will be viewed as one in a sea of many, and we will have little power in our relationships with our clients and prospects.

*T*he world does not need another general-ist design firm. There are enough full service advertising agencies and marketing communication firms. The world is drowning in undifferentiated creative businesses. What the world needs, what the better clients are willing to pay for, and what our people want to develop and deliver, is deep expertise. Expertise is the only valid basis for differentiating ourselves from the competition. Not personality. Not process. Not price. It is expertise and expertise alone that will set us apart in a meaningful way and allow us to deal with our clients and prospects from a position of power.

Power in the client-agency relationship usually rests with the client. His power comes from the alternatives that he sees to hiring us. When the client has few alternatives to our expertise then we can dictate pricing, we can set the terms of the engagement and we can take control in a manner that better ensures that our ideas and advice have the desired impact.

When the alternatives to hiring us are many, the client will dictate price. He will set the terms of the engagement. He will determine how many of our ideas and how much of our advice we need to part with, for free, in order to decide if he will choose to work with us.

It is first through positioning our firm that we begin to shift the power in the buy-sell relationship and change the way our services are bought and sold. Positioning is the foundation of business development success, and of business success. If we fail on this front we face a long, costly uphill journey as owners of creative businesses.

THE PURPOSE OF POSITIONING

Positioning is an exercise in relativity. Our goal when endeavoring to position ourselves against our competition is to reduce or outright eliminate them. When we drastically reduce the real alternatives to hiring our firm, we shift the power balance away from the client and toward us. This power shift allows us to affect the buying process and increase our ability to protect ourselves from having to part with our thinking for free, from having to respond to wasteful and inefficient tenders or requests for proposals (RFP), and to otherwise devalue our own offering or increase our cost of sale.

THE THREE STEPS OF POSITIONING

Positioning is strategy articulated and then proven. These components of strategy, language and proof are laid out here as the three steps we must take to build deep expertise and meaningfully differentiate ourselves from others:

1. We must choose a focus
2. Then articulate that focus via a consistent claim of expertise
3. And finally, we must work to add the missing skills, capabilities and processes necessary to support our new claim.

What we call *positioning*, others more serious about the business of their craft call *fundamental business strategy*. The first step – focus – is to answer the strategy question of "What business are we in?" Choosing the focus for our firm remains The Difficult Business Decision. Too often, we decide to not decide and so, in our minds, leave open the possibility that we may continue to do all things for all types of clients. In creative firms the world over – firms populated and run by curious problem solvers – the avoidance of The Difficult Business Decision remains the root cause of most business development problems.

We can easily complete the second and third steps of positioning once we have summoned the boldness to tackle the first. For reasons hardwired into the brain of an artist, however, most of us fail in this vital first step.

THE BENEFITS OF POSITIONING

We can measure the success of our positioning by gauging our ability to command two things simultaneously: a sales advantage and a price premium.

A Sales Advantage ↔ To possess a sales advantage means that when and where we choose to compete, we win more often than not.

A Price Premium ↔ To command a price premium means that when we win, we do so not by cutting price, but while charging more.

Winning while charging more is the ultimate benefit and key indicator of effective positioning, for price elasticity is tied to the availability of substitutes. The more alternatives to our firm, the less power we have to command a premium over our competition. If we do not win while charging more then it is likely we are attempting to run a business of ideas and advice from a position of weakness; or we are trying to compete outside of our area of focus; or we have avoided The Difficult Business Decision altogether and have chosen, by not choosing at all, to run a business without a focus or a fundamental business strategy.

Control ↦ Beyond the combined benefits of a sales advantage and a price premium, positioning brings us control in the form of increased ability to guide the engagement. We are hired for our expertise and not our service. It is a mistake to believe that the service sector mantra of "The customer is always right" applies to us. Like any engagement of expertise, we often enter into ours with the client not truly knowing what he needs, let alone recognizing the route to a solution. For us to do our best work we need to leverage our outside perspective. We need to be allowed to lead the engagement. We need to take control.

Our ability to control the engagement diminishes with time. Sometimes we lose control slowly and other times quickly, but we always lose it. It is important, therefore, that we enter the engagement with as much control as possible. Indeed, business development can be viewed as the polite battle for control. If we do not win it here, before we are hired, there is little point in proceeding.

It does not come easy to us to ask for control when we have little power in the relationship. To jockey for the power position seems at odds with our belief that we should demonstrate our enthusiasm for winning the business. We are optimistic, enthusiastic people, but it is time to admit that our enthusiasm has not always served us well.

WE ARE THE SUM OF OUR CHOICES

We are lucky to do what we love. And we deserve to be able to do it. But as business owners we need to accept that loving our craft is no substitute for making intelligent business decisions. Passion for design does not grant us dispensation from facing The Difficult Business Decision. Once we choose to make our passion our business, we take on responsibilities to our clients, families and employees. Among other things, those responsibilities include the need to generate a profit above and beyond the salaries we pay ourselves. It is from this profit that we build strength and create many forms of possibilities for ourselves and everyone involved in our enterprise.

Who among us, when faced with the question, "Would you choose to be weak or strong?" would choose to be weak? We face this choice on physical, emotional, spiritual, financial and other fronts. We face it in our personal lives and in business. Some choose to be strong because they wish to rule others. Some choose to be strong because they wish to help others. Some choose to be strong because they've experienced the alternative and never want to be weak again. What we choose to do with our strength is our decision, but as business owners we have an obligation to choose and then to pursue the path we have chosen. No one consciously chooses to be weak. In business, weakness is often a symptom of not making The Difficult Business Decision.

THE COST OF CREATIVITY

One of the hallmarks of creativity is a fascination with the new and the different. Properly harnessed, this fascination allows us to bring fresh thinking to old problems and ensure that our offerings to our clients are always evolving. Un-harnessed, our firm-wide desire for the new and the different can lead us to avoid The Difficult Business Decision. It can serve as a rationale for not having to choose a focus, for not having to eliminate competition.

We can choose to let our fascinations and passions go unbridled. We can choose to remain a "full service" firm doing all things for all people. This lack of strategy will make us relevant to everyone with marketing or communication needs. It will indulge our desires to do something different every day, and to make every engagement different from the previous ones.

When we make this choice, however, we invite all kinds of undifferentiated competition as well as some highly differentiated, specialized competition. We invite numerous alternatives to hiring our firm and we place the power squarely with the client. In this competitive environment we will never be the expert firm, we will never command the respect or margin we want, and we will never be free of the pitch.

We must recognize that as individuals we are inclined against the narrow focus that drives deep expertise, but we must also recognize that our business must have this focus if it is to prosper. We must see our protestations, rationalizations and justifications for not facing The Difficult Business Decision for what they are: *excuses*. While some make business success look easy, we know that the best rewards are the ones for which we've worked hardest. As creative people running businesses, the difficulty of deciding what business we are in is made harder by our inclination to preserve our options, to pursue something we've never done before, to reserve the right to do it differently next time.

THE PARADOX OF CHOICE

We stand in a room full of doors. As highly curious people, we want to see what is behind every door. This is our desire as artists – to satisfy our curiosity and solve the problems we haven't previously solved. On some level, however, we know that if we are to drastically reduce our competition and benefit from the resulting power shift, we must pick one door, walk through it and never look back. Our personal desire for variety is suddenly placed at odds with the fundamental need of our business to focus. Is it possible, however, that on the other side of the door we face there is not one long gray hallway, not one empty boring room, but more doors – more choices? Is it possible that what lies on the other side of the door is not the death of our creativity, sure to be snuffed by routine and boredom, but just enough focus to harness the full potential of our talents?

The answer, of course, is that it *is* possible, but we will never know for sure unless we walk through the door and close it behind us.

Fun and Money

Fun and money have long been the two reasons we go to work in the morning. If we are honest with ourselves we will admit that in the beginning it was mostly about the fun. We were doing the work we loved. Others validated our expertise by actually paying us for it. There were late nights of shared purpose with colleagues, everyone doing what needed to be done to wow the client.

We were kindred spirits all with the same passion for our craft. We celebrated our wins together and commiserated over the losses together. In those early days the studio was more college dorm room or rock 'n' roll tour bus than place of commercial enterprise.

Then suddenly, it wasn't fun anymore. Those that once inspired us became a burden. Employees became overhead. The late nights were too much. Somehow the money and the respect we hoped for never followed. The money, especially. For a long time we were in denial about the money. We didn't need it; we were having fun. Then, when we faced our reality and decided we did need money, we did so grudgingly. Now, we're tired of having fun and we're willing to admit we're in this, at least in part, for the money.

There are greater causes by which to frame an enterprise, and there are nobler metrics by which to measure the value of effort. But we cannot escape the fact that money is both a necessity in life and the most basic scorecard of success in business. Even if it is not the validation we seek, it is the most basic of tests that we must pass: *Is there a need for our efforts great enough to sustain and nurture them?*

Courage

The good news is that there is no fun like making money, because financial strength affords us all kinds of options in our business and personal lives. The path to financial strength begins with facing The Difficult Business Decision. There are some exceptions to the proclamation that we must specialize, but it is unlikely that we are one of them. Until we make a brave decision, success will elude us and we will look at the market and complain about the economy or the clients, all the while knowing that it was us. The problem has always been us, and our struggle with focus. We are at the root of our free-pitching problem and we alone have the power to free ourselves from the pitch. The client will not free us. Our trade associations can do little to help us. Our competition will not cease to give their ideas away for free.

The revolution we must fight is within. There is no enemy. We are victims only of a creative mind that makes choosing a focus more difficult for us than most. A lucrative future where our enterprise sustains us and nourishes our creativity is within our control. We must simply choose to take control, first by specializing and shifting the power back from the client toward us, and then we can begin to shape our future.

II

We Will Replace Presentations
With Conversations

We will break free of our addiction to the big reveal and the adrenaline rush that comes from putting ourselves in the win-or-lose situation of the presentation. When we pitch, we are in part satisfying our craving for this adrenaline rush, and we understand that until we break ourselves of this addiction we will never be free of the pitch. Presentation, like pitch, is a word that we will leave behind as we seek conversation and collaboration in their place.

*W*e in the creative professions are addicted to the presentation. We crave the sweaty palms, the increased heart rate and the heightened perceptions that come from standing at the precipice, addressing expectant faces and not knowing whether our reveal will elicit the approval and adulation we crave or the uncomfortable silence of failure. It is this not knowing – the soon to be hero or goat sensation – that propels us. We love presenting so much that we are willing to do it for free. This is the dirty little secret of our profession.

We will never be free of the pitch if we do not overcome our addiction to the presentation. Henceforth, we must work to eliminate the big reveal.

To wean ourselves of our addiction we must take the first step of changing our behaviour with our existing clients. Once we have accomplished this, the second step – changing the way we behave with prospective clients in the buying cycle – becomes possible. We will explore how to take these two steps, but first let us examine the hidden costs of pitching.

PRACTITIONER OR PERFORMER?
Even when we pitch and win, we lose. We devalue what should be our most valuable offering and set up the wrong dynamics between the client and us.

We must move away from the place where the client sits with arms crossed in the role of judge, and we take to the stage with song and dance in the role of auditioning talent. While both parties find the showmanship of our craft titillating, the practitioner's is a stronger place than that of the performer. It is this practitioner's position from which we must strive to operate. Practitioners do not present. Stars do not audition.

PRESERVING THE SURPRISE

A successful presentation requires surprise. It depends on a big reveal in the form of a key diagnostic finding, a dramatic strategic recommendation or a novel creative concept that is at odds with expectations or set against a backdrop of uncertainty. Preserving the surprise requires us to keep the client at arm's length and let our knowledge pool up behind a dam that will only be opened at the presentation. While we protest against the client's selection process that keeps us at bay and asks us to begin to solve his problem without proper collaboration or compensation, we often acquiesce, in part, because his process allows us to meet our need to present. In this manner, we allow – or even deliberately create – an environment that leads to a higher likelihood of failure in order to preserve the dynamics of the presentation.

At a time when we should be conversing, we are instead cloistered away preparing for the one-way conversation called the presentation. We behave this way in our engagements with existing clients, so when prospective clients ask us to bridge massive communication gaps by presenting to them instead of talking with them, it is only natural for us to agree.

STEP ONE: IMPROVING COLLABORATION WITH EXISTING CLIENTS

Making the big reveals small and reducing our dependency on the presentation requires us to work more closely with the client. This creates a challenge: how to invite him in without allowing him to drive? This delicate balancing act of bringing him closer without conceding control can only be achieved when we establish and communicate the rules of the engagement. Alas, another challenge: we've never been fond of rules.

When we do not clearly spell out how we will work together we leave a void that the client is quick to fill. Thus begins the erosion of the power we worked so hard to obtain by following the first proclamation. Nature abhors a vacuum. If we do not drive the engagement, of course the client will.

When we establish the rules of collaboration – to use first with our clients and then with our prospective clients – we ensure that all engagements begin with both parties understanding how we will work together.

The Rules of Collaboration

In our firm we will adopt the following policies that will allow us to bring the client closer without sacrificing control.

Strategy First ↔ We will agree with the client on the strategy before any creative development begins. By including the client in our strategic development processes, we will help ensure we never find ourselves presenting creative rooted in ambiguous strategies. We will not develop, nor share with the client, creative of any kind before the challenge has been diagnosed and the strategy prescribed and agreed to.

Continuous Reference to Strategy ↔ Immediately prior to presenting any creative, we will review the agreed upon strategy with the client. In this way we keep the discussion around the creative focused and measured against the strategy. Any time we come back to the client to share new ideas or concepts we will set the stage first by reviewing, once again, the strategy that guides us.

Freedom of Execution ↔ We welcome the client's input on the strategy and in exchange we ask him to grant us the freedom to explore various ways of executing it. This means we invite him to say, "That blue isn't bold enough to deliver on our core value of strength." But we explain that he is not invited to say, "Make it darker." Suggestions on this front are always welcome, but dictates are not. We value our clients' insight into marketing strategy, but we need the creative freedom to explore the destinations implied by the strategy. The client must ultimately approve of our recommendations, and be satisfied with the outcome, but he must also let us explore along the way.

Fewer Options of Better Quality ↔ When we present creative options we will strive to limit them to as few as practical. There is an inverse correlation between the quantity of creative options we present to the client and the confidence we have in their quality. When we present options we will recognize our obligation to recommend one over the others. We will be careful not to cede our expertise by asking, "Which one do you like?" We will direct all discussions around the creative back to the strategy and ask if we are accomplishing our goals. It is an abdication of our responsibility and our expert position in the relationship to share all of our endeavors with the client and then ask him to choose.

Only We Present Our Work ↔ Whenever our diagnostic findings, strategic recommendations or creative solutions are presented to anyone in our client companies, it will be personnel from our firm that does so. Our key client contacts may assist us, but our work does not get presented without our involvement. One of the benefits we bring to our clients is the advantage of an outside perspective, one that is not saddled with perceptions of bias or a hidden agenda. We will not allow proper guidance to be sacrificed at the altar of company politics.

If we are to replace presentations with conversation and collaboration, this combined act of bringing the client closer while continuing to lead the engagement is vital.

Our Misplaced Fear of Policies, Rules and Routine
Some of us will enforce the above rules of collaboration as policies and others will view them merely as helpful guidelines. For many of us, considering adopting policies is akin to a claustrophobic person considering entering a coal mine. One of the costs of creativity is the abhorrence of routine – the dislike of systematic ways of thinking and behaving. This characteristic of our hardwiring that contributes to our creative problem-solving abilities keeps us from establishing policies on how we work. It causes us to perpetuate the process void, that by implication, we invite the client to fill.

While we dislike routine, the client – and ultimately, any consistency of success – demands it. We must, therefore, reconcile ourselves with the fact that routine will be imposed. Once we accept this we can face the question, "Would we prefer to have routine imposed on us, or would we prefer to be the ones who take the lead and define the rules of the engagement?"

There will come a day when we are happy to hear from the client, "Ahhh, of course!" instead of the previously desired, "Oh – I love it!" On that day we will know that we have been working collaboratively and we will know that our addiction is behind us. Then we can work on removing the presentation from the buying cycle, taking us one step closer to eliminating the pitch.

STEP TWO: ELIMINATING BIG REVEALS IN THE BUYING CYCLE

At first, it's hard to contemplate the client hiring us without a presentation. The presentation seems like a natural and necessary step, until we ponder the question: "How would we conduct ourselves in the meeting if we were not allowed to present?" Without a presentation, all that is left is conversation – intermingled talking and listening un-separated by one party performing for the other.

Once we decide we will no longer pitch our ideas for free, what is left for us to present? Credentials? The most basic information about our firm already listed on our website? Surely we can convey these points in a conversation, without the need of a podium, projector or props.

Once we have eliminated our own need to present, the only reasons left to do so are the client's. But on this, the client shall not have his way. He may not recognize it yet, but the presentation serves neither our interests nor his.

Presenting is a tool of swaying, while conversing is a tool of weighing. Through the former we try to convince people to hire us. Through the latter we try to determine if both parties would be well served by working together.

The tone of a conversation, in which both parties endeavor to make an honest assessment of the fit between one's need and the other's expertise, is entirely different from the tone of a presentation, in which one party tries to convince the other to hire her. Presentations build buying resistance; conversations lower it.

Framed by Our Mission, We Pursue Our Objective

Let's consider for a minute what we are trying to accomplish in the buying cycle, in this meeting with the prospect in which we once played the role of presenter.

Mission: Position ↔ First, let us focus on our business development mission – our highest calling and purpose. *Our mission is to position ourselves as the expert practitioner in the mind of the prospective client.* We must resist the temptation to sacrifice our mission for money or other short-term gains. This mission should guide everything we do in the buy-sell relationship. It is a contravention of such a mission to try to sway someone to hire us through a presentation. This simple idea is radically at odds with what most of us have been taught. *It is not our job to convince the client to hire us via presentation or any other means.* As we will see in the fourth proclamation, convincing has no place in selling.

If we have failed in the first proclamation and we have not set ourselves apart from the competition, then we may never see the truth in the second. Obtaining the expert position and replacing presentations with conversations will remain an unachievable ideal.

Objective: Determine Fit ↔ While our mission is to position, our objective at each and every interaction in the buying cycle is simply to see if there is a fit between the client's need and our expertise suitable enough to take a next step. That's it. It is not our objective to sell, convince or persuade. It is simply to determine if there exists a fit suitable enough to merit a next step. *Our mission is to position; our objective is to determine a fit.*

In accepting any invitation to present in the buying cycle, we sacrifice our mission and reduce the likelihood of arriving at our objective.

Once we have obtained power through the sacrifice and hard work of following the first proclamation, why, for reasons other than our own personal needs and the profession's long ingrained habits, would we voluntarily give up that power through the sales pitch of the presentation?

The Roles That We Play

The dynamics of the relationship with the client are shaped early, before he hires us. Here we establish the role that each will play throughout the engagement. Most selection processes set up an audition atmosphere where one party commands and the other complies. We must never allow ourselves to be placed in this presenter/ complier role where the terms and next steps of the relationship are dictated to us. If we assume this lowly role that is offered to us early, we will never be able to exchange it for the loftier expert practitioner role that is required for us to do our best work.

In this manner, *how* we sell shapes *what* we sell. It impacts our likelihood of delivering a high-quality outcome and it affects the remuneration we are able to command for our work.

Now, the Truth About Presenting

Alas, you may have guessed that we will never be completely free of the presentation. That is not the goal of this, the second proclamation. *The goal is to be free of our own need to present.*

To be truly free of the pitch we must change the tone of these meetings with our prospective clients and move from the presenter/complier role to that of the expert practitioner. This we do as a doctor or lawyer would, through conversation and collaboration and not through presentation.

III

*We Will Diagnose
Before We Prescribe*

We will take seriously our professional obligation to begin at the beginning, and we will never put our clients or ourselves in the position where we are prescribing solutions without first fully diagnosing the client's challenge.

There are four phases in our client engagements:
1. Diagnose the problem/opportunity
2. Prescribe a therapy
3. Apply the therapy
4. Reapply the therapy as necessary

While it is common practice in the creative professions to prescribe solutions without fully and accurately diagnosing the problem, in almost every other profession such a sequence would render the professional liable for malpractice. Too often we are guilty of this flawed process and our clients are guilty of trying to impose such a process on us through the pitch. We owe it to ourselves and our clients to stand firm on this most basic of professional practices and to never agree to begin working on a creative solution to a problem that we have not fully explored.

In a process that pits multiple firms against each other and asks each to present solutions, the client does not have the time to invest in meaningful diagnostics with them all. So he abbreviates the diagnostic phase; he dictates the process, marginalizes it and proclaims that his self-diagnosis is valid enough for us to proceed.

But how many times have we proceeded based on the client's self-diagnosis only to discover that it was wrong? How many times has the client come to us stating, "I need X," only for us to discover that he needed Y?

It is more likely that the client's perspective will be wrong, or at least incomplete, than it is that it will be whole and accurate. *We know this.* Doctors know the same of their patients. Lawyers and accountants know the same of their clients. The customer is not always right. More correctly, he usually has strong ideas and a strong sense that he is right, but is locked into a narrow view and weighed down by constraints that seem to him to be more immutable than they really are. When the client comes to us self-diagnosed, our mindset must be the same as the doctor hearing his patient tell him what type of surgery he wants performed before any discussion of symptoms or diagnoses. Our reaction must be, "You may be correct, but let's find out for sure."

THE PRACTITIONER'S PERSPECTIVE

One of the advantages the outside expert brings is perspective. And one of the hallmarks of creativity is the ability to see problems differently, and thus find solutions others cannot see. To bring our perspective and problem-solving skills to bear we must be allowed time and freedom to diagnose the client's challenges in our own manner. Design is not the solution – *it is the process.* We cannot be effective, responsible designers if we allow the client to impose his process, or truncate or otherwise marginalize ours.

But let us not place all the blame on the client. Doctors face self-diagnosed patients as often as we do, but we are far more likely to proceed with such a flawed approach than any medical practitioner. We let the client dictate and drive the diagnostic process, usually because we have not bothered to understand, formalize and explain our own. We have not taken control on this issue. We have not correlated our likelihood of high-quality outcomes to working from a defined and meaningful diagnostic process. We have not made this case in our own minds and we have not made it to the client. So the client intervenes and fills the void in our own working process by deciding how much information and access we will be allowed in the pitch. Lacking our own process, we have little means to push back and argue for a better way.

To reverse the trend and live up to our professional obligation to diagnose first, we must map out and formalize our own diagnostic process. Then, when we are next in a situation where the prospective client is dictating to us, we must make the case that the consistency of our outcomes is rooted in the strength of our process, therefore we must be allowed to employ it.

THE NATURE OF SUCCESSFUL CLIENTS

In Aesop's fable "The Frog and the Scorpion," the latter approaches the former at the riverbank and asks for a ride across on the frog's back. But the frog is not so stupid as to readily agree to this favor, for surely once out in the river the scorpion will sting and kill him, as scorpions do. The scorpion protests that it would be silly for him to kill his carrier, as it would ensure his own death from drowning. The frog sees the scorpion's logic and agrees to the engagement. Once in the middle of the river the scorpion does indeed sting the frog, who, with his last breath, asks the scorpion why he has just killed them both. The scorpion replies that he cannot help himself. He is a scorpion and it is in his nature to sting.

The lesson here is not that clients are stinging scorpions that cannot be trusted. The lesson is that the most successful clients, whether owners or executives, have achieved their success in part because of their ability to take control – their ability to rise above and orchestrate others. *This is their strength; and even though it is not always in their best interest, it is in their nature.*

We are liable. Like the frog, we are the guilty party when we let the client control the engagement and dictate to us how we will go about understanding his problem. Just because it is in the client's nature to lead, does not mean he should be allowed to do so at all times. It only means that, like the scorpion, he will attempt to do what it is in his nature to do.

LEARNING FROM OTHER PROFESSIONALS

Other professionals do not suffer nearly as much as us in being dragged into engagements where the client or patient has been allowed to dictate the diagnostic process. Interestingly, many of us have discovered that these other professionals make the worst clients. The reason they avoid the problem we do not, and then create problems for us when they become our clients is the same: *they take control.*

Other professionals are taught to drive the diagnostic process or risk their professional credentials. When they become the client in the practitioner-client relationship they do what they always do: they attempt to take control. And we let them. The result is usually an engagement gone awry.

THE ROOT OF BAD ENGAGEMENTS

When we think back now on our worst client experiences we can see that most of them were rooted in this mistake of letting a dominant client direct the engagement, beginning with a self-diagnosis that we took at face value. Thinking we are in the same business as retail clerks, somehow convinced that there is truth, or even nobility, in the line, "The customer is always right," we took the money and did as we were asked.

When these engagements go wrong we cannot understand how the client can possibly blame us. "We only did as we were told," we rationalize. We see him as demanding and difficult. He sees us as irresponsible order-takers not worth the money he is paying. He responds with more angry demands and again we comply, giving him what he wants. The spiral continues until finally we part, each blaming the other.

If design truly is a process, then we will define and guard that process and we will walk away from those clients and situations, like the pitch, where the process is dictated to us, or where we are otherwise asked to propose solutions without a proper diagnosis.

THE POLITE BATTLE FOR CONTROL

The control that we need in order to do our best work includes the imperative to bring our own methodology to the engagement. Throughout the buying cycle we are constantly gauging whether or not the client recognizes and values our expertise to the extent that he is willing to grant us this control. Does he see us as the expert who merits the reins of the engagement, or does he see us as the order-taker supplier that needs to be directed?

Possessing our own formalized diagnostic methods, whether they are proprietary to us or not, goes a long way to our positioning in this matter. Like any other competent professional, it is reasonable to expect that if we address similar problems on a regular basis then we would have a formalized way of beginning the engagement. It follows that we would demand to be allowed to follow our own process and not readily agree to use one developed by the client or his procurement people. It also follows that when a client comes to us self-diagnosed, we would feel the same sense of obligation to validate that self-diagnosis as any other professional would.

A good client will begin to relinquish control once he has the confidence that the expert practitioner knows more than he does, *or has the tools to learn more*. Formalized diagnostic processes are such tools.

From here forward we will view the act of prescription without diagnosis for what it is: malpractice.

We will assert the professional's obligation to begin at the beginning and walk away from those that would have us proceed based on guesses or un-validated self-diagnoses.

IV

We Will Rethink

What it Means to Sell

We will acknowledge that our fear and misunderstanding of selling has contributed to our preference for the pitch. We will embrace sales as a basic business function that cannot be avoided and so we will learn to do it properly, as respectful facilitators.

*I*t is time for us to address our fear and mis-understanding of the basic business function of selling. We recoil from the "s" word because we see selling as the distasteful act of talking others into things. We see it as the act of persuasion. And while we are comfortable with our role as persuaders in a mar-keting sense – putting our clients' messages in front of groups of their desired customers – we bristle at such persuasion in the intimate setting of sales, where the interaction is more human and the product we are sell-ing is us.

If we are any good at what we do, we believe, then we should not have to talk people into hiring us.

A TALE OF TWO SALESPEOPLE

We have all been the customer in situations where the product or service we were presented with was not the best choice for us. In some of these situations we were aided by the respectful, considerate salesperson who also saw the poor fit between our needs and his product and so, appropriately, steered us away. But it is not this sales-person that we remember when we consider the necessity of selling our own services. For we have also been in these situations, but aided by another salesperson – the person for whom the transaction was all about him and his need to sell us his product. This second salesman sallied forth, intent on getting the sale, leaving us feeling violated and angry.

Perhaps the motivation of this second salesperson was rooted within his forceful personality. Maybe his incentives were aligned solely to sell to us rather than to help us. Maybe he was a victim of poor training, suffering from a misunderstanding of what it means to sell. But it is this second salesperson – the one at ease in the discomfort and adversity he created – that we conjure up when it is time for us to sell.

THE TWO FUNCTIONS OF BUSINESS

Making things and selling things are the two basic functions in business. For our business to succeed we must succeed at both.

It is true that if we are exceptional at the first we may experience times in the life of our business where merely being adequate at the second will carry us, but over time all things will revert to the mean. No matter how good we are there will be times when we are required to sell. We can wish this away, we can continue to avoid it, we can hide behind the pitch and kid ourselves that as marketers we are taking a more noble path to the same goal; but the truth is that until we embrace the fact that we are salespeople too, and we learn to master this craft as well, we will not achieve the success that we desire. *We cannot be in business without embracing selling.* We must, therefore, overcome the stereotypes and learn to do it properly – professionally.

Here, too, the pitch has not served us well. We have used it as a tool to avoid selling. As painful as it may be to give our thinking away for free and to act like puppets in the client-driven buying cycle, sometimes it is far easier to suffer the ignominy that at least allows us to practice our craft (even if for free) than to conjure up the sleazy salesperson and try to talk someone into hiring us.

SALESPERSON: FACILITATOR OF NEXT STEPS

The good news is that selling, when done properly, has nothing to do with persuading. It is not our job to talk people into things. The first salesperson had it right: selling is about determining a fit between the buyer's need and the seller's supply (our very objective) and then facilitating a next step. Sometimes the proper next step is to part ways, sending the client on to another provider who is better able to serve him.

We might argue that the high-pressure salesperson is going to sell more stereos than the respectful facilitator, but it is not stereos that we sell. We sell ideas and advice – the very contents of our heads – and so *how* we sell impacts what we are able to deliver. We cannot disappear immediately after the transaction is concluded, and leave the client to wallow in his buyer's remorse. After the close, our clients are stuck with us for a long time.

Yes, we must sell. But there is only one way we can afford to sell: the way of the respectful facilitator.

Let us think for a minute on how difficult the respectful approach is if we have not followed the first proclamation (We will specialize). If we have not specialized and set ourselves apart from our competition in a meaningful way then all we have left is convincing. Convince or pitch: these are the options of the undifferentiated firm.

A New Model for Selling

We have already established that our objective in each and every business development interaction is to determine if the fit between the client's need and our expertise is suitable enough to take a next step. This in itself implies the subsequent job of determining and then facilitating that next step. Let's explore a new model for doing so.

Proper selling can be distilled into three steps, based on the client's place in the buying cycle. These three steps replace the art of persuasion.

To sell is to:
1. Help the unaware
2. Inspire the interested
3. Reassure those who have formed intent

The first thing we must understand if we are to approach selling properly and respectfully is that the client's motivation, and by necessity, our role as salesperson, evolves as he progresses through the buying cycle. He moves from unaware of his problem or opportunity, to being interested in considering the opportunity, and finally, to intent on acting on it. As he progresses in this manner, our role must change from one of helping, to inspiring, and ultimately to reassuring.

BUYING IS CHANGING

The psychology of buying is the psychology of changing. Selling, therefore, is change management. The very best salespeople are respectful, selective facilitators of change. They help people move forward to solve their problems and capitalize on their opportunities. The rest talk people into things.

The next steps in this model of facilitating change are driven by the client's need to move forward to solve his problem, not by what we as salespeople have or have not done. The model does not ask, "Have we obtained a meeting?" It doesn't ask, "Have we presented a proposal?" The focus is on the client and whether or not he has recognized and begun acting on his need.

STEP ONE: HELPING THE UNAWARE

When we encounter a client who is unaware of any problem or opportunity that would require our services, what do our reflexes or previous training tell us to do? Convert the no into a yes? Try to obtain a meeting in order to attempt the conversion in person?

If we are narrowly focused experts then we should be able to succinctly articulate our expertise, and concisely describe to the client who we help and how, *over the phone*.

To request a meeting after the client has told us he does not see a fit is to admit that a) we need more time with him to explain what we do because we haven't been able to capture and communicate it succinctly, or b) we're looking to talk him into something.

That is why, when we find ourselves saying, "I'm going to be in the area and I'd like to come by to see you..." we cringe at the words coming out of our mouths. Such behavior creates buying resistance that we will have to overcome later in the relationship. It causes us to sacrifice our mission (to position ourselves as experts), and it creates the dynamics for an expensive sale that will see us poorly positioned to lead the engagement once hired.

No – for this future client, we must take the long road of helping him, over time, to see that perhaps he does have a problem. We do this primarily through the dissemination of our *thought leadership* – our writings on our area of expertise.

Real Thought Leadership

Over time, true thought leadership positions us as experts in our field and creates the opportunity for some of our thinking to trigger in the client the idea that perhaps his performance in a certain area could be improved.

The role of our thought leadership is to educate, not to persuade. The future client should be smarter for reading it, we should be smarter for writing it, and, one day, when the client does experience a problem in an area on which we've written, our guidance may be helpful to him in seeing the opportunity within his problem. Until that day, we continue to cement our position as leaders in our field through our writing. Experts write.

When we sit down to write about our area of expertise we will be confronted quickly with an assessment of our success in following the first proclamation. Are we adding to the millions of words that already exist on a subject? Are we retreading well-worn ground? (e.g.: *A brand is a promise,* or, *Is your brand authentic?*) Or, are we delving deeply into meaningful subjects for wisdom that truly helps?

Writing our way forward is a long-term approach that requires the patience of a farmer versus that of a hunter. But it is the only effective, respectful way with the client who says no and does not see the fit between his need and our expertise.

We can build a business with enough people saying no to us every week, provided many of them agree to subscribe to our thought leadership and we are diligent about future follow-up.

STEP TWO: INSPIRING THE INTERESTED

The unaware future client sits at his desk reading our thought leadership on an emerging media, technology

or school of thought relative to his business. His aware-
ness grows, and he begins to see that his organization is
lagging in this area. He assesses his situation. He begins
to gather more information. He considers the discomfort of falling behind. He looks to the future and now
imagines the benefits of being out front. He considers
the risks of taking action, weighing the pros and cons.
He is interested in the opportunity in front of him but
not yet intent on taking action.

The interested future client looks for inspiration to
move forward. This is where we as creative people excel.
We are among humankind's most natural inspirers. Our
work is inspirational. Our skill in commanding and
leading a room is inspirational. Our ability to come at
problems from previously unconsidered angles and our
passion for solving the problem not yet solved are both
inspirational. We excel here, in inspiring the interested.

Let us be clear: our goal with such a prospect is to inspire
him to form the intent to solve his problem; it is not
to inspire him to hire us. At this stage, hiring us is but
a possible future consequence of his deciding to take
action. Our focus needs to remain on the client, helping him to facilitate the change in himself that he is
considering.

Forms of Inspiration
Our portfolios are our best tools of inspiration. They
show the client what could be. They show him what

others have done. Our examples of our best work paint the picture of the beautiful world on the other side of his pain. Inspiration is the primary role of our website, our brochure, our sales collateral and our in-person portfolio review. It need not even be our own work that we show here to inspire the interested, just inspirational outcomes.

Misusing Inspiration
Like anyone, we play to our strengths. And, like anyone, our strengths become our weaknesses when we go to them too often.

When we get ahead of ourselves and attempt to inspire the unaware, we create buying resistance and set up the wrong dynamics. Trying to inspire someone who does not recognize that he has a problem is a recipe for defensiveness and resentment. Inspiration is something we must save for the interested.

STEP THREE: REASSURING THE INTENT
The interested prospective client sits across from us and, through our portfolio, views examples of organizations that have mastered the challenge he is now considering. Through our examples and our conversation, he begins to envision a future of wonderful possibilities. Inspired by what his company could become, he summons the resolve to commit to solving his problem. In this moment he says to himself, quietly, "I'm going to do this." His arrival at the decision triggers a change in

brain chemistry that brings a euphoric lift; the bigger the decision, the higher the lift.

He turns to us, excited and grateful for the strength we have given to move forward, and says, "This is fantastic! This is what we need! You people are great! I'll get back to you." And he means it. He truly means it.

The Emergence of Doubt

Our mistake is in thinking this is the last step. It is not. What goes up must come down. After only a few hours, the client's euphoria wears off and he slips into a hangover of doubt called buyer's remorse. Now he questions everything, including his decision to move forward. He considers all the things that could go wrong, all the reasons why this might not make sense.

As natural inspirers, our tendency is to do exactly the opposite of what is required at this moment. Playing to our strengths, we lean towards inspiration once again at a time when we should reassure.

It is not in the nature of most creative people to offer the reassurance the client seeks here. We tend toward excitement at a time when he requires calm. We speak of an organic approach to problem solving when the client would be soothed by the logic and consistency of hearing about our defined approach. We continue to talk big-picture when the client now needs to process sequentially and seeks to understand what the steps are that we would take together. He asks questions of the smallest detail – questions that seem meaningless and even odd to us, but are of the utmost importance to him in his quest for assurance that he is not about to make a significant mistake.

Alternative Forms of Reassurance

Closing – the last step in the buying cycle – is all about reassuring. Let us remember that when a future client has formed intent and asks us for a written proposal containing free recommendations or speculative creative, his primary motivation is fear of making a mistake. If we can keep this in mind and look past his request to his underlying motivation, then maybe we can find other ways to offer the reassurance he seeks. Most creative firms take these requests at face value and simply comply. Win Without Pitching firms offer alternative ways forward. Phased engagements, pilot projects, money-back guarantees and case studies framed in defined methodologies are among the many viable alternative forms of reassurance. *The key is to respond to the motivation and not necessarily the request.*

THE FOUR PRIORITIES OF
WINNING NEW BUSINESS

To follow the twelve proclamations and Win Without Pitching does not mean that we must always have our way. It is not our goal to replace the client's rigid and often ridiculous selection process with one of equal rigidity and absurdity. Let us be guided by the following hierarchy of four priorities of winning new business that will ensure we do not become overly rigid in our approach. The goal is to win. The preferred means is to not pitch. A firm that does not win will not last.

The First Priority: Win Without Pitching
We first strive to secure the business before it gets to a defined, competitive selection process in which we are pitted against our peers and asked to give our thinking away for free. This is easiest when the client sees us as the expert and reaches out to us first. It is also easier when we reach out to the client at a time early in the buying cycle, when he is unaware of any need; and we stay with him as he progresses through the buying cycle, at first helping over time, then inspiring when appropriate, and finally, reassuring at the end.

To Win Without Pitching is the ideal, but it is not always possible.

The Second Priority: Derail the Pitch
We often do not become aware of opportunities until late in the buying cycle – when the client has already formed intent, has already put a selection process in place and has reached out to numerous firms. In these examples our priority is to derail the pitch – to get the client to put his process aside and take an alternative first step with us. The twelve proclamations offer guidance on the principles of derailing the pitch.

The Third Priority: Gain The Inside Track

There will be times when, try as we might, we cannot derail the client's selection process. Some organizations' policies are too strong. Some clients are too unwilling – even when they do recognize and value our expertise. In these examples, we apply the same principles laid out here, but our priority is now to get an edge over the competition within the process.

When we do choose to participate in the client-directed selection process we should do so with the perspective that every competitive bid process has a preferred option. Somebody almost always has inside information or access to hard-to-reach decision makers. Sometimes the outcome is predetermined and the process is but a veil of legitimacy. Our default assumption should be that somebody always has the inside track. If we cannot Win Without Pitching, if we cannot derail the pitch, then we endeavor to be the one on the inside track. We begin to participate in the process but do so while constantly gauging whether the client recognizes and values our expertise. We ask for concessions. We ask for access to decision makers. We negotiate what we will and will not write in a proposal or show in a presentation. We measure the client's words, but more importantly, his behavior – his willingness to treat us differently – and if he grants us the inside track, then it may make sense for us to proceed.

The Fourth Priority: Walk Away

In the sixth proclamation (We will be selective) we will

discuss the need to walk away. There will be many times when it makes sense to do so; but for those prospects that would otherwise meet the parameters of clients we can best help, walking away is the fourth priority. We walk away when we cannot Win Without Pitching, when we cannot derail the pitch and when we are unable to gain the inside track. Good prospective clients who recognize and value our expertise will grant us one of the above. The others are not worth sacrificing our mission on in a long-shot attempt to out-pitch others, one of whom almost certainly has gained the inside track ahead of us.

WE ARE SALESPEOPLE NOW

In following this fourth proclamation, we will embrace sales as one of the two basic business functions, and we will go about this function in the manner of the respectful facilitator. We will look for those that we can best help. We will seek out those that see a fit between their needs and our expertise and who are willing to let us lead the engagement. And then we will facilitate the appropriate next steps: we will help the unaware, we will inspire the interested and we will reassure the intent. With this last group, we will look beyond their requests for proposals and free thinking to the motivations behind them, and we will suggest alternative ways forward. Those that see us as experts will grant us at least some of the concessions we seek and allow us to Win Without Pitching, to derail the pitch or to gain the inside track. From the rest, we will walk away.

V

We Will Do With Words

What We Used to Do With Paper

We will understand that the proposal is the words that come out of our mouths and that written documentation of these words is a contract – an item that we create only once an agreement has been reached. We will examine all the reasons we ask, and are asked, to write unpaid proposals and we will never again ask documents to propose for us what we ourselves should propose.

*W*hen we look back at the proposals we have written and we consider the engagements we have won, we can easily conclude that it was rarely the written document that secured the business. Those engagements we won were the ones for which we were best suited. The suitability of the fit was apparent to both parties throughout the conversations in the buying cycle. The written document did little to sway the decision.

Just as we are leaving behind the pitch, the presentation and persuasion, so too are we abandoning the written proposal and thereby freeing up the dozens or even hundreds of hours we previously devoted to it every year.

We have long been conditioned to think that the written proposal is a necessary step in the buying cycle. It is not.

The document that we write is the contract. It serves as public verification of an agreement we have already formed with the client *in conversation*. The agreement is an oral understanding that covers the scope of work, timeframe, budget and the basic terms of the engagement. While the agreement may be subject to minor details, all of these issues are addressed in conversation first. *The paper is produced only once the agreement has been reached.*

OVERINVESTING CREATES BUYING RESISTANCE

The buying resistance that we engender in the client is partly a result of the obvious investment we have made in the sale. When we spend hours on a lengthy written proposal, one that diagnoses and prescribes for free, it sends the message that we need the client's business. We clearly imply to him that he has the power in the relationship. Beyond giving him the upper hand, we also make it difficult for him to be honest with us. Let's face it, *No* is the second best answer we can hear. If the client does not see a fit between his need and our expertise, we want to hear so as early in the buying cycle as possible. The more heavily invested we appear to be in the sale, the less likely the client will tell us what he is really thinking. When he thinks we cannot bear to hear no, he will simply stall or defer or deliver a string of maybes. Most of the time, he will do so behind the shield of a request for a written proposal.

We want to operate from the practitioner's position where we have not overinvested in the sale, where we are not trying to talk the client into hiring us, and where we invite him to say no early and often. In this environment, there is no room for the written proposal, which, like the presentation, is a tool of swaying.

WHY THE CLIENT ASKS FOR A PROPOSAL

Even at first reading, the logic of this proclamation (We will do with words what we used to do with paper) seems obvious, almost irrefutable. This straightforward approach of using conversation rather than writing to determine a fit makes perfect sense for both parties, but it is rarely practiced in the creative professions. The written proposal is the norm and not the exception.

Let us explore the many reasons why the client asks for a written proposal and see how many of them are valid.

To Keep the Hordes at Bay

The over-supply of undifferentiated creative firms has necessitated a process that keeps the client from being overwhelmed. He uses the written proposal as a tool to help him. It allows him to keep the masses at arm's length and still give him something upon which to determine a next step. If we have succeeded in following the first proclamation and we have built an obvious specialized expertise, then we make it easier for the client to let us in. Otherwise, he will use the written proposal to keep us out.

We must embrace the challenge implied by the request for proposal (RFP). If we see the RFP as a tool for keeping undifferentiated firms at arm's length, then we will take up the challenge to break through the proposal process and gain validation that the client does indeed recognize and value our expertise. When he does not, he will use the proposal, and its supporting selection process, as a means of maintaining distance. The better clients, when they do recognize expertise, will crack open the façade of the proposal process and agree to a proper conversation. The question is one of merit: is the expertise of our firm deserving of such access?

This challenge aids us in determining very early in the process whether or not the opportunity is worth pursuing. For if the client does not recognize and value our expertise then we have failed – failed to build true expertise, failed to demonstrate that expertise or failed by pursuing an opportunity that is not properly aligned with our expertise. In most of these cases it is appropriate for us to retreat. We can do so without having overinvested in the opportunity. We can do so with our integrity intact and with possible future business opportunities preserved.

To Compare

In sorting through many similar firms, the client seeks to grid out their likenesses and differences. Undifferentiated firms gladly participate in this process. By not following the first proclamation, these businesses operate from positions of little power. Thus, all they can hope for is to win based on service (as demonstrated by compliance to the client's process), personality, price, or by beginning to solve the client's problem within the proposal. The process itself is an exercise in homogenization that reduces each firm to samples of its work, ill-informed guesses at possible strategies and hourly rates. True differences do not shine through in written proposals.

If we are pomegranates then we will resist being pushed into a process designed to compare apples to apples.

To Measure Value

Value = Quality/Price. The client's challenge in

determining the value of our services is that the quality of an idea not yet delivered is difficult to measure.
This leaves him with two options: he can over-weight
the decision toward that which he can measure (price),
or he can ask us to deliver the idea (for free) in an effort
to determine its quality.

By following the third proclamation (We will diagnose
before we prescribe) we demonstrate that our ability to
do our best work is rooted in the strength of our diagnostic and strategic development processes. A client
asking for unpaid ideas in a written proposal is like a
patient asking for a diagnosis and prescription from a
doctor he refuses to visit or pay.

The flaws of the proposal process are one more reason
we must see the request for a proposal as a challenge
to be met. Either we leverage the power gained by our
expertise to impact the client's process and replace the
proposal and accompanying presentation with conversation, or we walk away and leave this client to another
firm.

To Gain Inspiration
The most common, and costly, business development
mistake shared by creative firms around the world is that
of mistaking interest for intent.

Clients often ask creative firms for proposals before their
intent to act on their problem has been formed. In these

situations we must recognize that while the client is simply seeking the inspiration to help move him forward,
sending us away to write is not likely to achieve it. We
must learn to measure the client's intent; if his decision
to act on his opportunity has not yet been anchored to a
future date or event (a decent indicator of intent), then
the written proposal is not the tool to help propel him
forward. If the engagement has not yet moved from his
wish list to his to-do list, then it is still inspiration he
seeks.

We are better off in these cases exploring our previous
work for examples of inspiration, or examining with
him his competitor's work or other best practices from
further afield. Sometimes such explorations merit a
small paid discovery engagement, and sometimes they
are merely part of the conversations in the buying cycle;
but we must not mistake the seeking of inspiration for
the will to move forward.

To Stall
Sometimes the answer is no. Sometimes the answer
is probably not. And if this is what the client is really
thinking, then this is what we should be keen and able
to hear. But when we push too hard – when we pitch,
present and invest in a written proposal – we often make
it difficult for the client to be honest with us. In these
cases he will use the written proposal and its supporting
process to not say anything to us when he really would
like to say no. If the answer is no, we want to hear it;

therefore, we want to make it easy for the client to say it. It serves neither of us when we lob a written proposal over the fence and wait patiently for a reply.

To Shop Around for a Better Price
We are under no obligation to provide the client with a reference of services, process and price just so that he can find someone else to do what we would do, the way we would do it, but cheaper. *Res ipsa loquitur.*

RFP R.I.P.
Of all the reasons that a client might ask for a written proposal, none can withstand the stronger logic of having a conversation with an expert of few equals. When we fail to make this case then we must understand that we have failed in setting ourselves apart from the competition, or we have created buying resistance through our need to present or persuade. When we follow the earlier proclamations, we make following this fifth one possible; and in this way we continue to march from order-taker to expert, one step at a time.

Getting Paid to Write Proposals
One of our new mantras that we will repeat to ourselves and our potential clients is: *We do not begin to solve our clients' problems before we are engaged.*

Many times, the client's situation, or the probable solutions, are so complex or technical that we need to better understand the challenges if we are to propose and quantify responsible solutions. Such engagements demand that we begin our diagnostic work in order to present a plan. But let us not make the mistake of doing this diagnostic work for free. No – understanding and diagnosing the client's situation is vital to the success of any engagement, and it is our work here at the very front of the engagement that will largely determine whether we succeed or fail in our endeavors for the client. We must charge for this work.

Doctors charge for MRIs. Accountants charge for audits. Lawyers charge for discovery. And we charge for our diagnostic work as well, whether it is a brand audit or discovery session that we conduct ourselves, or outside research that we commission.

For these complex challenges in which we must diagnose before we can even begin to quantify a prescription, our clients pay us to write proposals via a phased sale that begins with a diagnostic. The outcome of the diagnostic phase is two parts: findings and recommendations. In our findings we deliver our diagnostic discoveries, and in our recommendations we include a plan to move forward, complete with timeline and budget. In this way, we get paid to craft the proposal those times when it is necessary to write one.

CONTRACTS AND PROPOSALS

Our proposal is indeed the words that come out of our mouths: "We propose to do X for you, over Y timeframe, for Z price." Once we have agreement on the proposal, then we write up the contract for signature. Let us be clear to our clients and ourselves: we are not in the proposal writing business. And let us make a promise to ourselves that we will no longer ask a document to do what we ourselves should do: *propose.*

VI

We Will Be Selective

Instead of seeking clients, we will selectively and respectfully pursue perfect fits – those targeted organizations that we can best help. We will say no early and often, and as such, weed out those that would be better served by others and those that cannot afford us. By saying no we will give power and credibility to our yes.

*M*ost of us do not suffer from having too few clients. The problem with our client roster is usually one of quality, not quantity. We sometimes attempt to compensate for the quality of our clients by adding more of them; but we know that having numerous small, unsophisticated or otherwise inappropriate clients is no reparation for having the right type and size of clients.

If we are to build a lucrative expert firm then we must regain this balance of a small number of high-quality clients. Once regained, we must accept that our client base will turn over and we must understand that this churn is healthy. Our client relationships should not be life sentences.

OUR BUSINESS DEVELOPMENT GOALS

Clients hire us at times of need. We generally solve the most pressing problems at the beginning of our relationships, and over time the nature of our work slides toward the tactical end of our offering. Thus, our positioning with the client changes. At some point we become less of an outside advisor and more of a partner, and then, ultimately, a supplier. Eventually we part ways. The transition is inevitable; the only variables are time and the point of departure.

The optimal engagement length will differ from firm to firm and from client to client, but we must embrace the idea that turnover is healthy, and the subsequent idea that our business development goal is to manage such turnover. If it is our desire to grow our practice, then we accomplish this by ensuring that the new clients we take in represent increased opportunity over that of those departing.

Selectivity is one of the defining characteristics of the expert. It builds credibility, reduces buying resistance and creates the conditions where it is possible to replace presentations with conversations.

A clear understanding of our goals – a small number of slowly revolving high-quality clients – makes it easier for us to adopt this selective approach. We will not win every opportunity, nor do we need to. From this we should take comfort and patiently go about finding those that we can best help in a manner that is more focused and less frantic.

RETREATING WHERE OTHERS ADVANCE

Clients can smell selectivity. It is one of the early cues that signal to them to drop their guard and partici-pate in meaningful discussions of fit, or raise it and retreat behind the protective cover of "the selection process" where they ask for credentials, proposals and presentations.

It is human nature to follow what retreats from us and to back away from what advances. Confucius famously said, "Speak softly and people lean toward you; speak loudly and they lean away."

Buyers prefer to be politely vetted by a seller who has clearly defined parameters of the nature of the work he will do, the type of client he will take on, and the budgets with which he will and will not work. The client's experience in dealing with the selective expert versus the enthusiastic generalist who barges headlong into every opportunity is night and day different. One invites him to advance; the other causes him to retreat.

BACK AGAIN TO THE FIRST PROCLAMATION

Selectivity begins with positioning – the very focus of our enterprise. Our public claim of expertise must describe who we help and how, and in this description those that would be better served by others should be able to select out. The client should be able to determine from a sentence or two whether our expertise is likely to meet his needs.

The narrower our claim of expertise, the more integrity we earn. By staking a narrow claim we build the credibility for the client to assume we have capabilities beyond our claim, whereas a broad claim generates the opposite reaction. The client knows the great difficulty of amassing broad expertise, and when such a claim is made he assumes our true expertise, if any, must be much smaller than what is declared. In his very first interaction with us, in reading the words on our website without having even met or spoken to us, he makes judgments on our integrity that will impact the dynamics moving forward.

The first proclamation lays the foundation for all others, including this, the sixth. If we have succeeded in specializing, then selectivity becomes easier for us.

IN PURSUIT OF NO

No is the second best answer we can hear. If the answer is no, we want to hear it as soon as possible, before we and the client unnecessarily waste valuable resources. When an opportunity first arises, therefore, we try to see if we can kill it.

This is contrary to how we typically act, but it is a powerful approach that lets us weed out poor fits early and eliminate those opportunities where the client would not hire us in the end (or those where we would regret that he did). If the opportunity is right and we retreat just a little, the client is likely to follow. The retreat-and-follow is an important test of how much the client recognizes and values our expertise. It tells us if he sees a fit and indicates to us the power we have to lead any engagement.

Our inclination is to avoid the questions to which we think we may not like the answers, but here again we must learn to fight our tendencies, demonstrate the selectivity and efficiency of the expert and march head-long into these conversations in pursuit of no. There are many common reasons why an engagement might not make sense: money, the nature of the client's need, his willingness to let us lead, geographic location, the depth of our experience. We want to develop the habit of putting on the table for early discussion these or any other concerns we, or the client, might have.

REVERSING THE DYNAMICS OF OBJECTIONS

The dynamics of objections are such that when one party raises them, it is incumbent on the other to address them. Our tendency is to avoid areas of potential objection, but they cannot be avoided forever. Eventually the client raises them and we are forced to address them. Such dynamics are easily reversed when we learn to raise the objections first and place them on the table for the client to address. Instead of waiting to hear, "You seem expensive," we might say, "I'm a little concerned about the ability an organization of your size has to afford us." In this manner we want to learn to lean into potential objections. If the objection is going to kill the deal, then let's kill it early.

BRIDGING THE EXPERTISE GAP

It is okay for us to accept work outside of our area of expertise, provided: we have the ability, we have the capacity, we can do it profitably and we are not deluded into thinking that such work immediately merits expanding our claim of expertise.

If we are well positioned then we will possess capabilities beyond – often well beyond – our declared expertise. When potential clients approach us with needs within our capabilities but outside of our central expertise, it is vital that we handle these enquiries with honesty. When our claim of expertise is broad, we are inclined to respond to such enquiries with what the client expects to hear: "We can do that!" This reply builds buying resistance and makes it difficult to replace presentations with conversations.

The target is not the market. We take precise aim at the smaller target and are happy to hit the wider market. Our claim of expertise should be a lot narrower than the sum of our capabilities.

When we encounter an opportunity within our capabilities but outside of our expertise, we owe it to the client to tell him that, yes, we can do this, but no, it is not why we are typically hired. We owe it to him to reiterate our claim and point out the gap between what he needs and what we do. From there, the client can make the decision to bridge the gap or not. He can decide that our experience translates to his need and that he would rather work with someone who is honest about her strengths. Or, he can decide to look for someone whose expertise more closely aligns with his need. If the gap is to be bridged, it's better if it is the client who does so. The dynamics of objections, and the need to reverse them, apply here, too.

On this point of accepting work outside of our expertise, let us remember that we never want to be enticed into competing for it. If the client bridges the gap and says, "I think you can do this," and it makes sense for us to do it, then we are within our rights to take the work. If his statement is followed by an invitation to compete for the work, however, then we are better to decline, point him in the direction of a firm better aligned with his need, and get back to looking for our next perfect fit. He may advance when we retreat, he may be worth following up with after he has spoken to other firms, but he may also disappear and never return. Regardless, we do not want to sacrifice our mission and be dragged into competing for work that is outside of our expertise.

THE PASSION DICHOTOMY

Who are we without our passion? It is an asset that drives us into the problems we solve. It is the motivational engine for finding the best solutions to the challenges we face. Surely, displaying such an asset in the buying cycle is advantageous? But here, too, we must beware and, to an extent, fight our natural tendencies.

Passion can be a tiebreaker when the client believes the level of expertise to be equal among his considered options. When we play up the tiebreakers of price, chemistry and passion, however, we tacitly imply that when it comes to measuring us on the most important variable – expertise – we are no better equipped than others in consideration.

We must be free to use our passion, without forgetting that it can easily become a liability. The client may view our display of passion as an invitation to take control and an admission that our expertise may be lacking. Let us use our passion but beware that we do not over use it and allow the client to use it against us.

SELECTIVITY DEEPENS WITH EXPERTISE

As our expertise deepens, so too does our ability to be selective. Expertise forces selectivity.

The generalist is drawn to the problem he has not yet solved. His curiosity trumps all else. He feels no discomfort in operating outside of his area of expertise because such an area is broad, shallow and loosely defined. He pursues with passion the new and the different.

When the transition is made however, and he becomes used to the benefits of deep expertise – when the client ceding control to someone deserving of such control becomes the norm – he will not be easily enticed back to operating from the powerless position of the generalist.

When given a choice to operate from the position of power that comes with deep expertise or to pursue work outside that area for clients who will not allow him to lead, the expert will refuse. He will refuse not because it is written here to do so, but because he will never want to retreat back to that place of generalist order-taker. He will be wary of situations in which he does not have confidence in his ability to find the best solution – in which the landscape and challenges are unfamiliar and he has to admit to his client, "I've never done this before."

Once he grows accustomed to operating from the position of the practitioner, the expert will take pains to ensure that his future clients grant him such a position. In this manner, his expertise will force his selectivity, but in the beginning it will not be so easy. Selectivity is something he must learn. He must put his passion in its place and walk away from those opportunities where he is not viewed as the expert.

And so must we all.

VII

We Will Build Expertise Rapidly

We will view our claim of expertise as a beginning and as a rallying cry for perpetual progress. Once focused, we will work to add to and deepen the skills, capabilities and processes from which we derive our expertise, and we will commit to the idea that continuous learning is mandatory.

*W*e address here the third of our three steps to positioning our firm. First we select a focus, we then articulate that focus via a claim of expertise, and finally we work to quickly add proof to our claim.

When we put our flag in the ground, heads turn. The competition, seemingly oblivious to us before, suddenly takes notice. Those that do not claim meaningful territory are rarely attacked. What is there to defend, after all? This is one of the indulgences of the generalist: it is an easier life. It is not as lucrative. It is not as fulfilling. It is, however, easier. Nobody attacks the unthreatening generalist.

The truth about the average human being is that, regardless of what he claims to want, he will avoid the difficult decisions and the undesirable tasks, even if they represent the path to the outcome or future he desires. The proven reality is that most people will change their desires, even their values, before they will change their behavior.

Now, the question we must face is, *are we most people?* Will we stay on the old comfortable path where we can avoid attack? Will we choose denial and continue to shape our beliefs to conform to our old behavior? Or do we have it within us to do what we know must be done to build an expert firm: a firm that delivers to our clients our best work, a firm that brings to us the fulfillment of a career well managed, and a firm that provides to our families the security and prosperity they deserve? Will we do what we know needs to be done?

MAKING THE CLAIM REAL

Putting one foot in front of the other, we begin by choosing a focus and articulating a claim (the first proclamation). Then we change the way we sell (proclamations two through five). We become selective about our new clients and the work we do for them (the sixth proclamation). And now that we have momentum and we begin to taste the benefits of expertise, here in the seventh proclamation we make a promise to ourselves that we will see how far we can go. We commit to deepening our expertise, rapidly and forever, so that we can find out just how good we can become.

From the moment we make the claim, we find ourselves in a race with no finish line. It is a race in which the greater our lead, the more we have to lose; therefore, the faster we feel we must run. *This is not the easy path.* Once we are on it, however, moving past the stationary generalists on the sideline, we realize we would not have it any other way. We would rather race to fulfill our potential than stagnate in unchallenged contentment.

THE IMPORTANCE OF PROVING OUR EXPERTISE

A claim is just a claim; anyone can make one. Our claim of expertise helps us break through the clutter of competition and gain attention at the very first interaction with the prospective client. But from then on, it is incumbent on us to prove our claim. The further we progress into the buying cycle, the more the proof of our expertise aids us. Without proof, we find ourselves having to pitch – having to begin to solve the client's problem as proof of our ability to solve his problem.

The proof that we desire to build, and that our future clients need to see, is rooted in our skills, capabilities and processes. These are things that we must never cease to build – assets to which we must never stop adding. Let us explore some means we have available to us to deepen our expertise.

Starting With Focus

The good news is that the very act of focus is likely to build depth. If we were to take two people of similar intellect and abilities and charge the first with building a business with a broad focus and the second with building a business with a narrow focus, we would find that the second person would build a depth of expertise exponentially greater than that of the first. He could not help but do so, for when we narrow our field of thought we think deeper. We need not be smarter or more creative than our competition, only more focused. Focus is powerful, but it is just the first step in building deep expertise. Other steps follow.

The Requirement to Write

Writing gets us found. Writing helps to cement our position as experts. Most important of all, writing about what we do is the fastest way to deepen our knowledge. Writing at length on our expertise drives us into the deep crevices of our territory. As focused experts, we benefit from repeated observation of the same challenges. Writing is the tool that helps us formalize our thinking on these observations. It forces us to tighten our arguments and therefore our understanding. Writing might not come naturally to us, it might be painful at times, but the rewards are significant and the exercise is mandatory. If we are to be experts we must write.

The skills we must possess or acquire in order to succeed in a differentiated creative enterprise are: consulting first, writing second, artistry third. The problem-seeing and problem-solving skills of the advisor, along with the ability to lead others through the engagement, trump everything else. Writing follows, for writing both proves and deepens our expertise. The artistry, increasingly, is the commodity. It is inexpensively acquired from those that neither have, nor attempt to cultivate, the first two skills. We must take control and we must write.

Formalizing How We Work

If we were paid to dig a ditch of a specified depth, width and length, our first attempt would be completed at quality X, in timeframe Y. If we were to dig a ditch of those same specifications every day, we can assume that the quality of our output would increase and the time required would decrease. Repeated observation and problem solving is bound to improve our quality and efficiency.

We can also reasonably assume that over time, through trial and error, we would happen upon an efficient approach that allows us to deliver at quality and speed *with consistency*. In almost any of our repeated endeavors, it is the strength of our processes that drives the consistency of our outcomes.

If we want to build deep expertise we must take pains to document how we work, to define how we will work in the future and to continuously refine and improve our approach. Working from a defined process leads to the very consistency of quality that a potential client tries to discern late in the buying cycle, when our role is to reassure. Nothing reassures the client more than him drawing the powerful inference that *little variability in process equals little variability in outcomes*. Every one of the firms he is considering can demonstrate an ability to do great work, but the question he wants answered before he buys is: "How do I know I'm going to get their best work?" When we are able to demonstrate strong processes, the client can decide for himself the implications of our processes on the consistency of our quality.

Training and Empowering
If we have no meaningfully defined processes, then there

is not much to train our people on. But once we commit to defining and improving how we work, then we must commit to training our people on such methods.

Training and other forms of individual professional development are vital, for a creative firm either has a culture of continuous learning or it does not. We must make the commitment that in our firm all our people will feel compelled to keep up with their associates and excel past our competitors. When our new employees come to work for us they must feel as though the learning never ends and the pace of learning never lessens. We race together.

We build a culture of continuous learning by hiring for skill, by developing it through training, by empowering our people to form their own professional development plans that we will approve and fund, by holding them accountable to these plans, and, most importantly, by leading with our own example. We go first, and set the example of pace and determination required to be part of our enterprise.

ALL WILL NOT FOLLOW

While creative people have a proclivity for generalist tendencies that allow them to explore the new and the different, most will select a path of deep expertise once it is shown to them and they have experienced the benefits. Without that experience, not all will be convinced to join us on our journey.

The culture of tolerance and inclusiveness that we've always had in our firm still applies, but now it applies only to those willing to pull their weight. When we choose to follow the twelve proclamations and make the transition from order-taker to expert, we commit to the idea that perpetual learning and continuous improvement are mandatory. Everyone involved in our enterprise must buy in, pull his weight and push the rest of us as we push him. Those who do not will be shepherded on to other firms where the collective desire to realize potential is more in line with their own.

THE ONE WHO EDDIED OUT

We know the principal who eddied out – the owner of the creative firm who enjoyed early success for many years only to have that success leave him for good. He started on his own during good economic times or with one large benefactor client and he rode that current for years. Then things changed. The economy turned or the client moved on and the principal's easy success vanished.

For years now he sits wondering what went wrong. What did he do to deserve such misfortune? What he cannot, or will not, see is that his misfortune is rooted in his early success. He was not forced to make the difficult decisions early, so when faced with them late he remained certain that the decisions and the effort could be avoided, and success could be had the old way once again. Now clients no longer beat a path to his door, and he blames the market or he laments that times have

changed in a manner he cannot comprehend, for reasons he cannot see.

As others move past him, making the brave decisions and
doing the difficult work, he remains, with his reminis-
cent stare, bobbing in the calm at the side. He stays there
for us, as a reminder of what we will become if we ever
stop learning, if we ever give up the race.

VIII

{THE EIGHTH PROCLAMATION}

We Will Not Solve Problems

Before We Are Paid

Our thinking is our highest value product; we will not part with it without appropriate compensation. If we demonstrate that we do not value our thinking, our clients and prospects will not. Our paying clients can rest assured that our best minds remain focused on solving their problems and not the problems of those who have yet to hire us.

A pitch-based business development strategy devalues our thinking and emphasizes the more commoditized parts of our offering. If we do not value our thinking, the client will not. He uses many cues to try to ascertain our value. He looks for signs from us of how we value ourselves. How can we diagnose and prescribe for free one minute, and later ask for hundreds or thousands of dollars for similar thinking?

We must strive for a consistency in our behavior that says we know our own worth and we will not be led into selling ourselves short. We must address our own negligence in standards around this behavior, and simply agree that there is a line that separates proving our ability to solve the client's problem from actually solving his problem. We shall not be lured into crossing over this line before we are paid.

This pervasive challenge of giving our thinking away for free is easily remedied. It is as simple as deciding we will no longer do it, writing this commitment into a policy statement, and then stating to the client with polite conviction, "It is our policy to not begin to solve our clients' problems before we are engaged."

It is irresponsible of us to use our identity as artists as an excuse for not forming business standards and policies. Clients lay policies on us as though they were law and we respond with preferences and inclinations. No – we must respond with policies of our own. We encounter far less client resistance when we preface our requirement with the words, "It is our policy that…"

FREE THINKING IS NOT JUST CREATIVE

Many of us weigh the free-pitching problem and feel proud that it does not affect us. "We don't do speculative (spec) creative." But our designs are merely the application of our strategy; and our strategy, when arrived at responsibly, is rooted in a thorough diagnosis. Each of the phases that precedes design or any other application work has a value at least as high as the application. Like creative, this thinking that precedes it should not be given away for free.

The line that separates proving our ability to solve the client's problem from actually solving his problem begins at the diagnosis. We correctly collect preliminary diagnostic information in the buying cycle in order to assess the client's situation and make a determination of our ability to help. *But we should not progress so far as to share our diagnosis with the client before we are hired and appropriately paid.* Beyond that, we certainly should not be prescribing strategy without proper diagnosis and compensation. Free pitching is free thinking, period.

ONCE HIRED

Our need to not begin work without appropriate compensation does not end once the client commits to working with us. The transition from intent prospect to new client takes place through a series of steps, each an escalation in his commitment. While we do not doubt his word when he speaks it, we must remember that he is not fully committed until he has parted with his money. *Every client reserves the right to change his mind until he parts with his money.*

The escalation of commitment begins with a private one, when he says to himself, "I'm going to do this." From there he moves to shared commitment when he says aloud to us, "Let's do this." He then further escalates his commitment by signing his name to a legal document, be it a contract, letter of intent or memorandum of understanding. But even now he is not truly committed. It is not until he has parted with his money that he is fully committed to moving forward with us; and even then we will still have to reassure him through the inevitable period of buyer's remorse.

We must recognize this escalation of commitment as a natural series of steps, and simply ensure that we do not begin to solve the client's problem until he has completed all of them, the most important being the last: payment. One third to one half of the fee portion of the engagement is appropriate, or even the entire fee for the first phase in a phased engagement.

There is no need for us to be tentative about stating our requirement for a deposit before we begin working for the client. We simply say, "We'll get started as soon as we receive the deposit, as is our policy for all new clients."

We need not apologize for being responsible business people. Never again should we find ourselves attempting to clarify issues of payment after we have begun working on the engagement. This is the simplest of business tests, one for which there is no longer any excuse to fail: for all new clients, we will be paid in advance.

We Will Address Issues of Money Early

We will resist putting ourselves in a position where we have overinvested in the buying cycle only to find the client cannot afford to pay us what we are worth. We will set a Minimum Level of Engagement and declare it early in conversations so that if the client cannot afford us, both parties will be able to walk away before wasting valuable resources.

*L*et us commit to memory the Win Without Pitching rule of money: *Those who cannot talk about it, do not make it.*

We claim to have been raised in a family or a culture where it is impolite to talk about money, but we know this is only a half-truth, don't we? In every culture it is impolite to talk about money *in a personal setting.* Just as ubiquitous as this rule is its corollary: in every culture it is considered a sign of poor business acumen to avoid talking about money *in a business setting.* We must recon-cile these two conventions and not confuse social mores with sound business practices. One of the goals of our enterprise is to make money; therefore, we must form the habit of talking about it early and often.

THE STRESS OF MONEY CONVERSATIONS

How often have we found ourselves deep into a business development opportunity, heavily invested in time and other resources, only to learn at the end that the client's budget was far below what was required for us to do the job? How is it that we get so far with such a gap in vital information? How is it that we allow ourselves to do so much work without first having a meaningful conversa-tion about the financial fit between both parties?

The client has a budget, or at the very least, budget limi-tations, and we should have our own parameters that define our minimum client size. With each party having such criteria, it becomes easy to determine as early as practical if there is a financial fit. But for many of us, it is not easy: money conversations are a source of stress.

When we take stock of the stress in our life, it is easy to see that almost all of it is caused by things that are either out of our control – or, more often, things that are within our control that we are avoiding. Stress is caused by the things we do not do. The root of this money stress is not in the conversations themselves, but in not having them when we know we should. Overcoming this stress begins with deciding that from here forward we will talk about money early and often. As soon as the opportunity arises we will lean into the discomfort of the topic, deal with it immediately and eliminate the stress from the subject. In time we will learn to do this with ease.

A Minimum Level of Engagement

By following the sixth proclamation (We will be selective) we agree to be more purposeful about the new clients we take on. We agree to establish the criteria that define with whom we will and will not work. Included in such criteria is budget, and specifically the fees that such budget would represent. When we commit to deliberately managing a slow, steady churn of a small number of clients, we commit equally to the idea that each new client must be of a certain size, representing a certain amount of fee income. We owe it to our prospective clients to share such fee expectations with them as soon as appropriate.

The annual fee minimum that we require becomes our Minimum Level of Engagement. It is an approximate number (usually somewhere around 10% of our total target fee income for the year) that we use as a tool to quickly weed out poor financial fits, to escalate discussions of short term tactical projects into discussions of long term strategic engagements, and to help us begin the money conversation early.

Soon after a need is initially determined, it is incumbent on us to let the prospect know that we only work with a small number of new clients every year and therefore can only add clients that will spend at or above our Minimum Level of Engagement. We are not looking to the client for an iron-clad commitment on this point, we are simply saying, "This is the size of client it makes sense for us to work with, so if you decide at some point that you would like to work with us, we ask that you be prepared to commit to fees at or above this level over the year."

COMMITTED BUT FLEXIBLE

The Minimum Level of Engagement is a powerful tool that we want to commit to using often, but without being overly rigid in its application. There will be times when we choose to waive our minimum, but let us not confuse the prerogative to waive it with the necessity for using it in conversation. We want to develop the habit of routinely sharing our Minimum Level of Engagement in every first discussion of an opportunity with a new prospect, while always reserving the right to waive it, if appropriate. Waiving it without mentioning it doesn't count. Such behavior is simply a failure to follow our own parameters of selectivity.

ON PROJECT WORK

As selective experts, it is not in our interest to pursue project work that is tactical in nature or well below our Minimum Level of Engagement. This does not mean we do not take on project work from time to time. Obviously, we undertake project work for existing clients with whom we have larger, more comprehensive and strategic relationships. We may choose to take on new project work if it meets certain criteria, such as, if we have capacity, if we can do it profitably, if it does not impair our ability to obtain more appropriate strategic work from the client in the future and if we do not have to compete for it.

Project work is a byproduct of pursuing a small number of more meaningful engagements. We use it to fill gaps in capacity, but it is not the mainstay of our practice. If we were to accept even half of the project work that comes to us, then we would find ourselves aimlessly building a tactical firm burdened by too many small clients and projects, with the commensurate challenges of poorer financial reward and less fulfillment. We will refuse more project work than we accept, but from time to time we will accept it. It is here that we would waive our Minimum Level of Engagement.

WAIVING OUR MINIMUM LEVEL OF ENGAGEMENT

When we do choose to waive our minimum and accept either project work or the occasional more meaningful strategic engagements just below our minimum, we can still benefit from its power by keeping it in place as an obstacle that we may or may not move aside.

Delivering our Minimum Level of Engagement early teaches us of the client's ability to afford us. If we find that the client does not meet our minimum, but for other reasons, may still represent a lucrative opportunity, we can simply follow up with language such as, "Before I say no, let me ask you a few questions." This keeps the minimum in play and lets us continue to gather information to make an assessment of the fit. In this way, we better manage the dynamics of the buying cycle.

If we determine the fit is suitable and we decide we would take this client on as one of our few exceptions to our minimum requirement, we must ensure that removing the minimum is the last thing we do before accepting the engagement. We never want to be in a position where we agree to waive our minimum only to hear, "Great, we'll send you an RFP," or, "Now we need to meet with a few more firms."

We use our Minimum Level of Engagement like any other objection that we raise early for the client to overcome. Like the others, we reserve the right to remove it. This is the power of no. When we use it, it helps us measure and improve our place in the relationship, and it's only as permanent as we need it to be.

WALKING AWAY

One of the functions of business development is to keep bad clients or other poor fits out. Like the gatekeepers at our clients' companies, we must establish who is allowed in for meaningful discussions and who should be gently guided away to a more appropriate relationship with our esteemed competitor. The fastest way to efficiencies in our business development approach is to unabashedly uncover important information early and use that information to make an honest and practical assessment of a fit. The answer to the question, "Can and will the client afford us?" is vital information that we must resolve to uncover as soon as possible. Walking away from those that cannot pay us what we are worth lowers our average cost of sale and preserves both our positioning and any future business opportunities with the client.

Discussing money early is an easily formed habit that, once acquired, helps us better make the decisions that shape the future of our practice.

X

We Will Refuse to Work at a Loss

We will build our practice one profitable assignment at a time. Excepting our carefully selected pro bono engagements and the occasional favor to our best and longest standing clients, every project will generate a profit that recognizes our expertise and the value we bring to our clients' businesses.

*W*e will strive to win while charging more and thus validate our expert positioning. If we are not accomplishing this feat, then we have not yet succeeded in implementing the earlier proclamations.

We must dispossess ourselves of the notion that we can operate on thin profit margins at the beginning of a new client relationship and then work to increase those margins over time. We know that profit margin, like power, only diminishes with time.

The tenth proclamation builds on the others before it: the need for diagnosis before prescription, the need for selectivity, the need to discuss issues of money early. Not only will we meet our obligation to diagnose before we prescribe, but we will selectively work for those clients willing to pay us for such an approach.

WE ARE HIRED TO BEGIN AT THE BEGINNING

Like the medical professionals that our four-phase model of diagnose, prescribe, apply and reapply suggests, our highest value offering is our ability to bring new perspective and understanding to our clients' problems. Success at each phase depends on getting the earlier ones correct. The first two phases of diagnose and prescribe represent the strategic portion of the engagement – the thinking phases that precede the doing. Our strength in these first two phases is what sets us apart from our competition and keeps the commoditizing forces of the profession at bay. The thinking that precedes and wraps our doing is our value-added differentiator. It is the basis of our deep expertise. Our opportunity for profit margin in the engagement is greatest in these first two phases and diminishes from there.

No client will willingly allow us to reverse this natural trend and command more profit margin as time goes on. We must admit that an approach that sees us sacrifice significant margin to win business with hopes of making it up later is rooted either in naivety, a false agreement with a client who is telling us what we want to hear, or in our own dishonest intentions of hoping to find profit that is not visible to the client.

A key test remains to win while charging more. When we win by charging less, price becomes our positioning that we wear like an albatross with that client forever: we become the price shop.

ON DISCOUNTING

In our enterprise there will be no loss leaders. As experts, we will not discount with new clients today for the opportunity to make money tomorrow. We will save the use of discounts for our best and longest serving clients at times when they need our support.

Legitimate price negotiations are fair game. If, from time to time, we decide that it makes sense to cut price to win the engagement, we must ensure we never cut so deep as to jeopardize its profitability. By seeing that every engage-ment is profitable, we ensure that our firm is profitable. By allowing an engagement with a new client to begin unprof-itably, we set up what is almost certain to be a relationship of mutual discontent.

Alternatives to Discounting

We may negotiate from time to time, but before we cut price we will ensure we have explored all the alternatives.

Guarantees ↦ Clients may attempt to negotiate because they are unsure of the value of our services. In these situations we can consider guarantees as alternatives to discounting. Not guarantees of return on invest-ment – for too many variables remain out of our control. Not guarantees on our entire spectrum of offerings – for they may be used against us late in the engagement. It is appropriate to guarantee the first phase – diagnosis and prescription – of a phased engagement in order to reassure the client of the value of moving forward with us. There is far less risk in this guarantee than there is in pitching free ideas and hoping to get paid.

Terms ↦ Clients may see the value of our offering but attempt to negotiate based on their inability to pay. In these situations, before we discount we should consider offering favorable terms that let the client pay over time.

Holding Our Ground ↦ Sometimes clients will see our value and will be able to afford us, but will negotiate to get a better price nonetheless. Often, negotiating success in these cases goes to the party most comfortable talking about money. The one with the least emotional baggage on the subject will do better at holding his ground. By following the ninth proclamation (We will address issues of money early), we work to ensure that party is us.

Two Rules for Discounting

When we have explored the alternatives and still we choose to discount, we will adhere to two rules:

We Leave it to Last ↔ First, we will ensure that cutting price is the last thing we do. We will search for and address all other objections before we agree to discount. In one final sweep before we agree to accept less we will ask, "If we were to agree to this price, is there anything else to stop us from deciding to work together right now?" If no objections or next steps remain, then we can cut our price and take the engagement. If there remain steps to be taken or objections to address, then we will do so before we discount.

We Put it in Writing ↔ Second, we must ensure that such discounts are clearly identified in all written documentation, including contracts, estimates and invoices, in order to remind the client of the true value of our services. Our failure to abide by this rule will almost certainly cost us in the future as the client "forgets" this proper value and references only what he previously paid. By recording our discount in all price documentation in this way, we ensure that such a discount does not set a precedent for new pricing moving forward.

OUR PRO BONO CLIENTS

We will build a lucrative expert practice one profitable engagement at a time, and then use the strength of our firm to help those that need it most. For these carefully selected charity clients, we will work for free.

We will leave to our competitors the unseemly practice of working for charities for free in the beginning in hopes of up-selling them to paid services. We will let others choose their charities based on the business connections they hope to make in the boardroom, but not us. We will treat charity as charity and not confuse it with business development.

Among those charities whose causes align with our values, we will work with the neediest, commit to them unselfishly and sacrifice any opportunity to benefit financially from this work. We will thus give ourselves the courage to ensure that every for-profit engagement is indeed profitable. This relieves the burden of the mushy middle of barely-profitable clients and quasi-charitable causes.

This is the emancipating duality of pro bono work: it is the charity we must do, and it gives us the courage to turn away work that would be only marginally charitable or questionably profitable.

Every one of our for-profit engagements will bring us profit. Our carefully selected pro bono clients will bring us nothing but fulfillment. We will leave to our competition those clients that would neither bring us profit nor merit our charity.

Using Pro Bono Work to Build Expertise

In the early days of a firm, there can sometimes be little foundation on which to build expertise. Here, pro bono – or even deeply discounted work within the selected field of focus – might be required to build that expertise. In these cases, there is no shame in being upfront with a prospective client about working cheaply or for free to amass expertise. Such an approach is valid, for a period of time. If we truly are trading profit for expertise building, then we will be honest and direct with our client about it. To do it quietly is to employ the generalist tactic of competing on price.

XI

{THE ELEVENTH PROCLAMATION}

We Will Charge More

As our expertise deepens and our impact on our clients' businesses grows, we will increase our pricing to reflect that impact. We will recognize that, to our clients, the smallest invoices are the most annoying. Through charging more we will create more time to think on behalf of our clients and we will eliminate the need to invoice for changes and other surprises.

*B*y following the money proclamations – getting paid first (VIII), talking money early (IX), refusing to work at a loss (X), and now, charging more – we develop a confidence that attracts better clients and weeds out poor fits without wasting resources. Proper employment of our Minimum Level of Engagement helps in this regard: thrifty clients are repelled and quality clients are attracted.

In boldly charging more than our competitors, we advertise to our prospective clients that we have confidence in our ability to deliver high quality outcomes.

As we get better we will charge even more, until we find that equilibrium that captures the appropriate remuneration for the value of our services. Our premium pricing will cost us clients from time to time; but if we are not losing business on price occasionally, then we are not charging enough. Conversely, if we need to win on price, we are not setting ourselves apart as experts.

Like our competitors, we too will use pricing as a positioning tool; but unlike them, we will strive to demonstrate higher pricing and thus benefit from all its positioning implications. Where others talk of their "competitiveness" on this front we will march headlong into the subject, following the ninth proclamation (We will address issues of money early), and boldly explain that we are likely to be more expensive than other options under consideration.

We will invite the client to tell us that he would prefer to work with a more affordable firm. We will not apologize for charging more; it is fair compensation for the increased value we deliver as experts. It lets us improve our offering by giving us the means to reinvest in ourselves and, most important of all, it almost certainly improves the outcome and the experience for the client.

PROFIT IMPROVES SERVICE

When we take on an engagement with thin margins and then we encounter a problem with the engagement – from our doing or not – we are left with little ability to fix the problem. Healthy margins give us the wherewithal to fix mistakes, earn trust and build loyalty with our clients. In this way, our most profitable clients get our best service. It does not happen the other way around. Superior service does not improve profit; *profit improves service.*

The test for this is the ringing phone. When we look down and see the profitable client's name, we are happy to pick up. When the unprofitable client calls, we cringe. Our clients know whether they are getting the best from us, but they rarely know why. Failing to charge enough leaves us little room to move and creates discordant dynamics with our clients. All of this affects the quality of our work and our reputations as reliable advisors.

Every client on our roster deserves our fullest attention, our best service and our commitment to fixing mistakes.

For us to deliver this to them they need to deliver to us the profit margin that will allow it. We need to accept nothing less. Healthy profit margin is vital, for sometimes the right thing to do is to give some of it back in order to correct a bad situation. The implied understanding is: we will be paid well and in exchange we will take care of the client. We will make all the little problems go away.

How many client relationship problems could have been avoided or fixed if we had charged properly? How many of our clients could we have done better for simply by commanding a little bit more money?

THE DEATH OF THE CHANGE ORDER

The change order represents most of what is wrong with our business model and our client relationships. Firms like ours are not fired over the large invoices for strategic work; they are fired over the small invoices for tactical work. It is the change order that creates the resentment that builds until the relationship snaps.

Would we eliminate the change order and the client resentment that comes with it if we had it in our power to do so? Such an achievement is possible. When the client allows the expert firm to take control of the engagement and charge more, he does away with the injustice of a new invoice every time a small tactical change is requested. Is this not a tradeoff that quality professionals and better clients would make?

TIME OR THINKING: WHAT ARE WE SELLING?

We sell our thinking but we do ourselves a gross disservice in selling it by the hour. The surest way to commoditize our own thinking is to sell it in units of doing: time. Later in the engagement, when the strategy work has been done and we are deep into implementation work, the client buys our time. It is our thinking, however, that separates us from our competition and forms the basis of our ability to premium price. When we charge for this thinking by the hour we undo much of the work of the previous proclamations. *"How much an hour?"* we hear the client think. *"How many hours?"* When we employ commodity pricing we invite commodity comparisons, regardless of the value we deliver. The defining characteristic of a commodity is an inability to support any price premium. If we cannot win while charging more, then we must face the reality that we are selling a commodity.

Strategy is Not What but How

While our engagements follow the four phases of diagnose, prescribe, apply and reapply, it is the outcomes of the third and fourth phases that are the deliverables the client seeks. Our strategy – diagnoses and prescription – is *how* we do what we do. The strength of our strategic processes, rooted in our deep experience and systematic thinking, is what ensures our high likelihood of a high-quality outcome. This is the basis of the premium we command, *therefore we should not be charging for it in units of time.*

We must price our upfront work, right up to the first creative deliverable, in big round numbers that end in zeros, and thus clearly imply that our pricing for these services has little to do with the hours it takes to deliver them.

For the reapplication work that follows, we are free to charge by the hour. When our clients buy our thinking, however, they need to understand they are not buying it in units of time. It is not until we cease to sell these strategic services by the hour that we can truly charge more.

PREMIUM PRICING IMPROVES COMMITMENT

We never want our clients to be in situations where it is easy for them to decide to not take our advice. Any time someone hires an outside expert, the ultimate outcome he seeks is to move forward with confidence. What is the value of good advice not acted upon? Yes, it is our job to tell him what to do, but that is often the easy part. We are equally obliged to give him the strength to do it.

We are not meeting our full obligations to our clients when we make recommendations that they find easy to ignore. The price we charge for such guidance should be enough that our clients feel compelled to act, lest they experience a profound sense of wasted resources. There must be the appropriate amount of pain associated with our pricing. This implies the need for our pricing to change as the size of the client changes. Larger organizations *need* to pay more to ensure their commitment.

Larger Clients Get Greater Value

Another reason larger clients must pay more is they derive greater financial value from similar work we would do for smaller organizations. To charge John Doe Chevrolet what we would charge General Motors for the same work would be irresponsible of us. The larger client pays more to ensure his commitment to solving his problem and to ensure his commitment to working with us – *and he pays more because we are delivering a service that has a greater dollar value to him.*

Reinvesting in Ourselves

Of all the investment opportunities we will face in our lives, few will yield returns greater than those opportunities to invest in ourselves. Price premiums give us the profit to reinvest in our people, our enterprise and ourselves. The corporations that we most admire are the ones that invest in research and development. We must follow their path. While others get by on slim margins, winning on price, we will use some of our greater profit margins to better ourselves and put greater distance between our competition and us.

Better Margins Equal Better Firms and Better Clients

On these many levels, charging more improves our ability to help our clients and increases the likelihood that we will deliver high-quality outcomes. It allows us to select the best clients – those that we are most able to help. Like leaning into the discomfort of money conversations, charging more might not come naturally or seem easy, but it is better for everyone, including the client, and so this too we shall learn to do with confidence.

XII

{THE TWELFTH PROCLAMATION}

We Will Hold Our Heads High

We will see ourselves as professional practitioners who bring real solutions to our clients' business problems. We will seek respect above money, for only when we are respected as experts will we be paid the money we seek. This money will allow us to reinvest in ourselves, become even better at what we do and deliver to our families and ourselves the abundance we deserve.

*T*oday, we in the creative professions find ourselves standing at a crossroads. On the one side, the process of design is finally being seen as the last great differentiator of businesses and economies; while on the other, the outputs are increasingly seen as commodities.

Technology and oversupply are combining to rapidly widen the gulf between the commoditized tacticians who now bid their services against each other online, and the expert practitioners who command significant fees for leading their clients to novel solutions to meaningful business challenges. The middle is disappearing. The need to choose a path is being forced upon us. If we continue to choose not to choose, the decision will be made for us, and we will be pushed down the commodity road where we will reside with thousands of other order-taker suppliers who will never be free of the pitch.

This is not a bad time to be forced into decision. The world is waking up to the idea that the challenges of both businesses and societies are challenges of design, creativity and innovation. The opportunity for us to have a meaningful impact on the world has rarely been larger.

SUSTAINING THE DREAM

From the very beginning, we were driven by some bold ideas. We were taught in school that the artist's place in the world was special. We were encouraged by our teachers and fellow students to live the dream, to surrender to our passion and revel in the nobility of our craft. Absent among these early encouragements, however, was any discussion of money or basic business practices. We were never taught to address the very issue of sustainability: how to ensure our practice thrives so that we may keep doing what we love for as long as it moves us.

There *is* nobility in our craft. There is a special place for those with our skills of seeing and creating. When we commit to building an enterprise around these skills, however, we must also commit to acquiring another set of skills that will allow our enterprise to thrive. Let us dream the dream but also be practical enough to make The Difficult Business Decision, and let us make a habit of barging headlong into the sometimes-undesirable tasks that must be done if our enterprise is to thrive. Dreams alone are not enough.

SELECTIVITY IS POWER

When we express our resentment for the client who does not value us, we are really expressing our self-loathing for not being able to walk away from him. We must accept that the bad clients and the ridiculous selection processes are not going away. Those that expect us to work for free as a means of proving our worth are not suddenly going to disappear. It is, after all, the client's money. He can employ any means he likes to select someone to help him, no matter how absurd or insulting. We can only control how we respond. The power we wield is the power to walk away.

There is always another, better opportunity behind the one facing us. If we cannot see it, we must at least believe it. In following the twelve proclamations we will leave the poor clients to our competitors, and in this way acknowledge that the free-pitching problem is never going away – it is only going away from us.

AMONG THE PROFESSIONS, BUT APART

While we strive for the respect that is easily assigned to the other professions, we must acknowledge that we are different. We aim to bring to our enterprise the business savvy that they bring to theirs, but we know we can never be them. We didn't choose our craft; it chose us. And we were never in this for the money. Even though we can no longer deny the importance of it, it is still not money that drives us. Profit is the proof of the worth of our enterprise. It validates our gifts and gives us the strength to make our mark on the world, and *that* is all we have ever wanted. Like all creative people, we only seek to create, and in doing so, somehow change the world.

We aimed this high in the early days of our practice, but then got buried in the minutiae of running a business. Perhaps we started to believe the lie that to get new clients we had to sacrifice a little bit of self-respect. We occasionally found ourselves groveling. Too often, we did adequate work for poor money for people who didn't value us. The acts of creating and problem solving bring us fulfillment, but the struggles of running a creative business often push us further from our lofty goal. How can we harness our gifts to change the world if they are so common or undervalued that they must be given away for free?

THE RETURN OF VISION

What we once saw as a battle with our clients we now see as a journey of personal transformation. One proclamation at a time, the fog lifts, the path becomes clearer and soon success appears possible, then inevitable.

THE GIFT WE MIGHT GIVE

We possess something that most others do not. We see what others cannot. We can conceive what does not yet exist. At our very best, we have it within us to lay out the future and lead people to it. When we imagine ourselves at our best, we can see again the change we might bring to the world. We can see the power we have to move people and organizations. At our best, what problem can we not solve? In banding together with others like us, what change can we not bring about?

We are the people who see. The cause of our revolution is not to rid the world of free pitching; it is to build a business that allows us to rise to the highest heights possible and make an impact on the world that is larger than us.

We will master the twelve proclamations so that our enterprise may sustain us and nourish our creativity. We will do great work for those who respect us and pay us our worth. From our rewards we will use our gifts to lift our families, inspire our communities and influence all of humankind. Focus, selectivity, respectful selling, continuous learning and conquering money – these are but steps on our path.

ACKNOWLEDGEMENTS

The contributions of dozens of my clients fill these pages. To all of them I am grateful for the trust they have shown in me and for all they have taught me.

More than anyone else, three colleagues have helped form my thinking. Pauline O'Malley (paulineomalley.com) showed me that selling could be done respectfully and logically. Her teachings are everywhere in my work and her voice continues to guide me. The ideas of David C. Baker (davidcbaker.com) – mentor, colleague, publisher and friend – also appear throughout these pages. David's impact on my work is so profound that I no longer attempt to keep track of what is mine and what is his. Cal Harrison (beyondreferrals.com) has been an invaluable collaborator, reviewer, teacher and long-time friend. I have been shaped by, and have stolen from, all of them.

Three writers offered valuable feedback on this manuscript, and guidance on navigating the writing process. I am indebted to fellow Kaslovians, Holley Rubinsky and Randy Morse. I don't pretend that the third, Mark Twain, would be happy with this final version, but in twice rising from the dead to warn me against publishing the manuscript prematurely, he helped ensure that I am happy with it.

My wife Colette Enns did what she always does: supported me unblinkingly throughout the book, the business and life. Here, words fail.

ABOUT THE AUTHOR

Blair Enns is the founder and CEO of Win Without Pitching, the training and coaching organization for creative professionals worldwide. He is the author of *Pricing Creativity: A Guide to Profit Beyond the Billable Hour* (RockBench, 2018), available only at pricingcreativity.com, and is the cohost (with David C. Baker) of the podcast *2Bobs: Conversations on the Art of Creative Entrepreneurship.* Blair lives with his family in Kaslo, British Columbia, Canada.

winwithoutpitching.com
pricingcreativity.com
2bobs.com
@blairenns

CREDITS
Cover and book design by Brian Sooy, Aespire
aespire.com
Sheffield Village, OH

Handlettering by Brian Sooy

TYPEFACES
Titling and Body Copy: Mrs Eaves OpenType
by Zuzana Licko, Emigre®

Initial Caps: Æ Prosperity™ by Brian Sooy,
Altered Ego® Fonts, alteredegofonts.com

Printing: Color House Graphics, Grand Rapids, MI